World Ecology for Young Readers

HOW PLANTS BEGAN

written and illustrated by Mel Hunter

WORLD PUBLISHING

TIMES MIRROR

NEW YORK

Published by The World Publishing Company. Published simultaneously in
Canada by Nelson, Foster & Scott Ltd. First printing—1972. Copyright © 1972
by Mel Hunter. All rights reserved. Library of Congress catalog card number:
79-184029.   ISBN 0-529-04533-8 (Trade Edition); ISBN 0-529-04534-6
(Library Edition).   Printed in the United States of America.

For almost three billion years after the planet Earth took its place in the family of planets around our Sun, there was no form of life moving in its empty waters, its barren mud, and its clouded stormy skies. Space research has shown that tiny particles of many chemicals which are the building blocks of living cells are scattered throughout space between the stars. Perhaps the new planet swept some of them into its upper clouds, as it spun among the dusty reaches of our still-forming galaxy of stars. More and more of these tiny chemical particles accumulated in the gathering drops of rain, which poured down from the skies to fill the canyons below.

Just how some of the chemicals combined to make the first tiny "living" cell we do not know; but such living particles did form in the waters of Earth, about two billion years ago. They "lived"—in that they could split apart into two identical cells just like the first. Each cell could then grow and split again. Though too small to see, they soon spread through all the waters of the planet. No living enemy existed to slow their quick multiplication. For more than a billion years, they were the microscopic lords of the Earth.

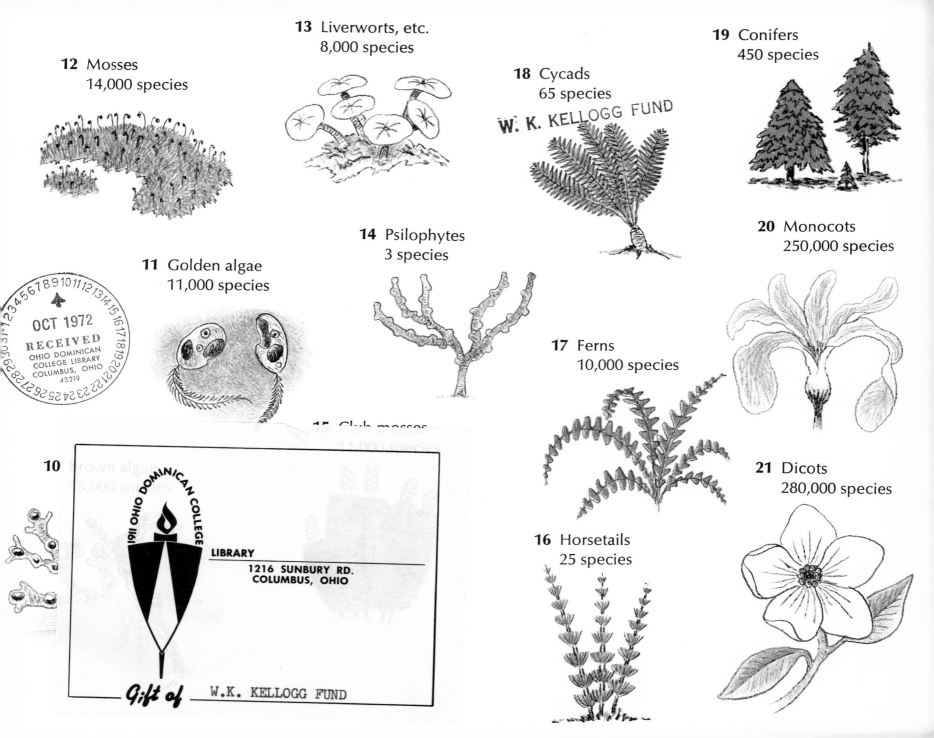

12 Mosses
14,000 species

13 Liverworts, etc.
8,000 species

18 Cycads
65 species

19 Conifers
450 species

14 Psilophytes
3 species

11 Golden algae
11,000 species

20 Monocots
250,000 species

17 Ferns
10,000 species

15 Club mosses
11,000 species

10 Brown algae
5,000 species

16 Horsetails
25 species

21 Dicots
280,000 species

The silent pine, standing in the shadows and dark colors of its forest world, has lived unchanged for so many millions of years that we humans are like newborn children beneath its branches, trying to decipher the history of Earth. The plants of our world carry much of that history hidden in the genetic adaptations they have made to the changing seasons, winds, and waters, while endless numbers of species of struggling animal creatures have appeared, lived, and died off forever beneath their branches. Mountains have reared up toward the heavens, only to be worn away by wind, rain, and ice to become flat plains again. Oceans now wash over ancient grasslands, and high desert plateaus were once the lair of deadly sharks. Ice sheets a mile thick have ground across half the face of the planet many times.

Still the plants have survived and prospered. In size and numbers, they far outweigh all other life on Earth. We need them. And now, as we bulldoze the planet with our technology, they need us.

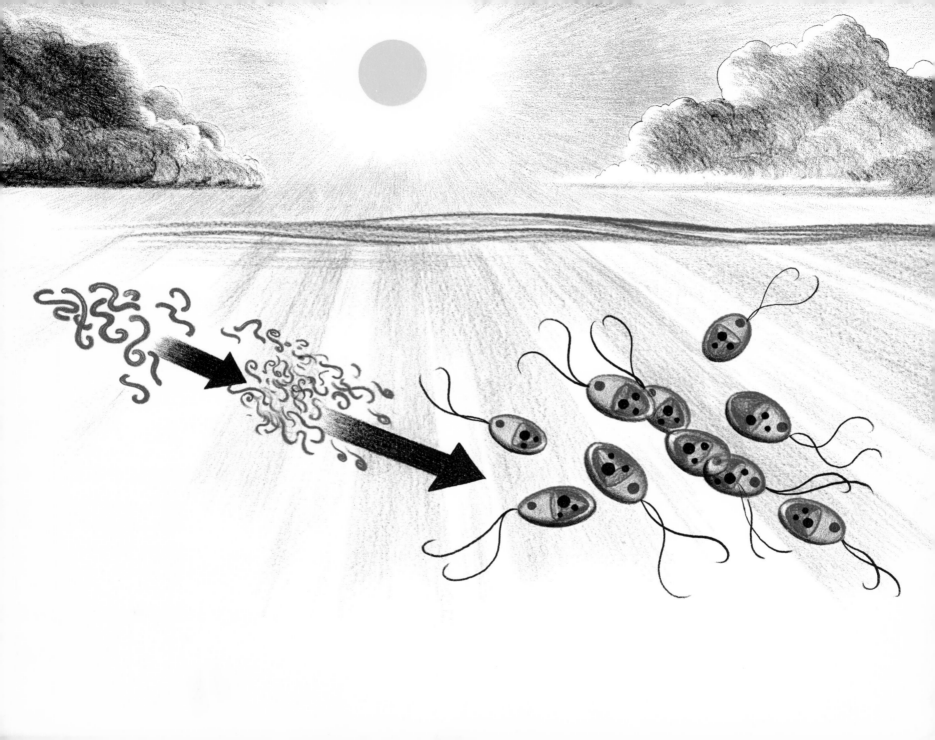

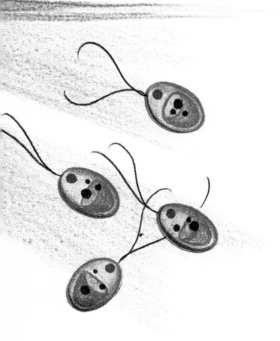

Millions of volcanoes spewed forth water vapor, chemicals, poison gases, and mountains of ash and debris. The seas became salted with more dissolved chemicals, as torrential rains washed down from the barren slopes. The skies gradually cleared. Deepening oceans developed layers of water differing in saltiness and temperature, just as the oceans are layered today. These new conditions encouraged gradual change in some of the bacterial forms. New types could feed, grow, and reproduce more efficiently in each layer, thus overwhelming their neighbors. Some changed even more. By 600 million years ago, new forms called Chlorophyta had appeared. These could wiggle their tiny whips to swim and were able to use the energy of sunlight to make food from the chemicals dissolved in the water around them.

Unchanged, they still exist today in most any pond or stream.

Following the appearance of the Chlorophyta, using their green particles of chlorophyll to make food, many different kinds of tiny organisms began to develop. Some formed partnerships with other species, so that by cooperating they could survive better than each could alone. Some formed a combination of chlorophyll-rich foodmaking plant cells, surrounded by tough outer cells of the fungi family, which protected them from damage. These colonies of fungi and plants are called the Lichenes. Such tough new forms of living cells were not killed when the receding waters of some tidal pool left them stranded on the exposed and empty land. Rapidly, they spread inland from the swampy seashores, combining and recombining in new forms which could live in heat and cold, dry or wet, at high or low altitudes. Wherever they thrived, their accumulating remains began the long slow process of fertilizing the soil of Earth. They provided the organic humus which other plant forms must have to live. More complex plants soon evolved to survive the harsh changes of life out of the sheltering waters. Yet the simple molds, mushrooms, and lichen groups themselves have survived unchanged for almost 500 million years.

By 400 million years ago, many new types of plants were finding
life in the open air more successful than life beneath the water.
Some were descendants of the great brown algae seaweed,
which grows up to a hundred feet long in shallow waters. Some
developed the ability to manufacture stiff woody cells to raise
themselves upright, high above the ground on the first true stems.
In this way, many new kinds of plants escaped from under the
shading leaves of their neighbors in the mud. Absorbing more of
the life-giving sunlight through their leaves, they grew even faster.

Club mosses, liverworts, horsetails, and others of these very early
plants can still be found today, surviving almost exactly as they were
millions of years ago. But when they first arose from the muddy tidal
seashores, they sheltered only a few giant three-foot scorpions, small
horseshoe crabs, and other primitive little animal creatures.

The next great step in plant evolution brought forth the first true leaves. With many broad leaves to catch the Sun's rays, plants were able to grow many times faster and larger. Soon there were great tangled jungles of giant ferns, club mosses, horsetails, and other spore-producing plants. Their lives were short, and their roots were shallow and weak like those of the modern palm tree. But they grew furiously in the hot, wet climate of this time on Earth. Trillions of such plants lived and died, pressing down on the rotting remains of those fallen beneath their clutching roots. The thickening layers of dead plants were squeezed beneath more and more weight from those above, until they became the hardened coal we burn today. A seam of coal now twenty feet thick, deep in the ground, is the squashed graveyard of millions of dead ancient plants like those shown here.

There were no men alive on Earth to see these gigantic club-moss "trees" sprout up a hundred feet in a few short years, or to dodge the huge insects that buzzed among their branches. But scientists have found the petrified remains of these plants, showing every tiniest leaf and vein, deep in the seams of coal mined beneath the ground. The huge plants of these Coal Age forests reproduced mainly by spores, in the same way as the ferns and mosses of today.

A typical fern plant develops thousands of little spore-producing spots on its leaves or stems. Millions of tiny spore cells are dropped into the winds. A few of these catch and germinate on properly moist soil and grow to form a tiny plant completely different from the parent fern. This plant forms two tiny organs on the underside of its leaves. One produces male sperm cells, which must travel through the wet soil to find and fertilize the female egg cell in the other organ. Once fertilized, the egg begins to divide over and over again into new cells, eventually producing a new fern plant.

As long as the weather is mild and the soils wet, the spore method of reproduction works wonderfully well. But the Earth gradually changed and grew cooler and drier. Spore plants began to lose ground to newer forms. Today, most ferns, mosses, fungi, and other sporophytes are quite small.

Labachia

Dimetrodon, one of the first dinosaurs, had a brain the size of your middle finger, though he weighed half a ton. He was the most advanced animal of his era on Earth, 220 million years ago; yet at his feet fell the perfectly shaped seed cone of the tree called Labachia. Labachia was one of the first plants which produced seeds, but it was already almost exctly like most of the great coniferous trees you see every day: the pines, spruces, firs, larches, cedars, and hemlocks.

Seeds were a great advancement over spore reproduction, because seeds could lie dormant for many months, even years, in the ground until the perfect conditions for growth appeared. The great family of seed-bearing conifers managed, by adaptation, to survive droughts, floods, fires, earthquakes, and the vast sheets of glacial ice that destroyed countless species of animal life forever. Only man, in cutting the forests of Earth faster than they can grow, threatens to end their long, long life on Earth.

Sugar pine

As the age of the great reptiles progressed, producing ever-larger and more complicated animal forms, the plants of Earth also changed. The first true flowers appeared. Their bright colors and sweet scents attracted insects to crawl through blossom after blossom. The tiny pollen grains rubbed off on their legs, bodies, and wings, and unknowingly they carried them directly to other blossoms, where the pollen was again brushed off to fertilize the waiting seeds. Plants with flowers could reproduce with far less pollen than those which depended on the winds and luck to deposit pollen grains in direct contact with the female organ of another distant plant of the same species.

Tyrannosaurus, last and greatest of the meat-eating dinosaurs, and Triceratops, one of the most capable plant-eating forms he attacked, both disappeared more than 70 million years ago; but the flowering trees which gave them camouflage and food survive today in every woodlot. The wildflowers they trod underfoot have modern descendants in every meadow. The flowering grasses that nourished Triceratops were the ancestors of the wheat, corn, rye, rice, barley, and other grains we eat today.

The great advantages which flower-bearing plants possess have been offset by some of the wind-scattering pollen plants. These produce such incredible clouds of wind-borne pollen that fertilization of the eggs of nearby plants of the same type is almost certain. A pine tree produces no flowers, but many large female, egg-bearing cones and smaller pollen-scattering cones. The tiny yellow pollen grains which these release are scattered in every direction on the winds. Eventually, a few may fall on the opened, upturned scales of a female cone, where the eggs are then fertilized, thereby producing seeds.

In a few months, the growing cone turns slowly over from its
weight and hangs down. When the seeds are fully ripe, the cone
scales open wide, and the seeds fall to the forest floor.

One bee can fertilize hundreds of blossoming tree eggs, as
it crawls busily from flower to flower, collecting pollen to make honey.
Some species of flowering plants attract bees and bumblebees;
others attract various honeymaking wasps and hornets, butterflies
and moths. Some attract meat-eating flies and beetles by producing
a scent which smells like spoiled meat. But whatever the variety,
all are helped by the passing insects to produce their seeds.

Plants continue to evolve as the ages of Earth's history progress. Pollen from one plant sometimes fertilizes the egg of a similar plant of a different color, or shape, or size. Gradually, more and more types of each plant are produced. Some of these changes are useful to the plant and continue; others, instead, are harmful, and the plant so changed dies out.

A simple example of plant change can be shown by cross-pollinating red and white four-o'clocks. The seeds thus produced grow into plants on which all the blossoms are pink. If these pink-blossomed plants are again cross-pollinated, the average results for each four offspring plants will be as shown. Obviously, if cross-pollination continues regularly, there will be many more pink than red or white blossoms. Other changes show up in the same fashion, gradually becoming more and more the normal appearance of the plant—or less and less.

Tulips have large simple stamens covered with male pollen grains
and a center pistil that contains the ovaries holding the plant
eggs. When a bee carries pollen grains to the next blossom, one
or more of the grains may catch on top of the pistil as he lands.
This pollen grain later grows a long thin tube which enters the
neck of the pistil and finally touches an egg deep inside. The egg
receives male sperm from the tube and begins its growth by
cell division. It becomes a seed, which later falls to the ground.
Examine the parts of a flower for yourself, to learn how its life
cycle continues through birth and death—and birth again.

Almost all plants convert sunlight into the energy they need for growth and reproduction. They draw up water, together with many dissolved minerals and chemicals, through their root systems into the veins which carry this vital liquid upward to the leaves. There, chlorophyll cells are able to use the energy of the Sun's light to break down and recombine the incoming chemicals into the sugars and other nutrients which provide food for the growth of all the plant's cells. In this process, called photosynthesis, the plant absorbs carbon dioxide gas from the air and gives off oxygen in return. Falling leaves and branches are digested and returned to the soil by other plant organisms that live in the soil nearby and by plant-eating animals. The rich humus thus produced is needed by other plants for the chemical building blocks of life.

All the oxygen in every life-giving breath has been put into the air by the plants that have lived and died through the ages in the seas and soils of Earth. Without the trillions of oxygen- and humus-producing plants that renew our air and soil, neither plants nor animals nor man can live. The animals and plants of Earth have evolved together, and each now depends on the other for survival. Man, the dominant animal who changes the face of the Earth as he pleases, must not—in the name of progress—thoughtlessly destroy the plants that give him life.

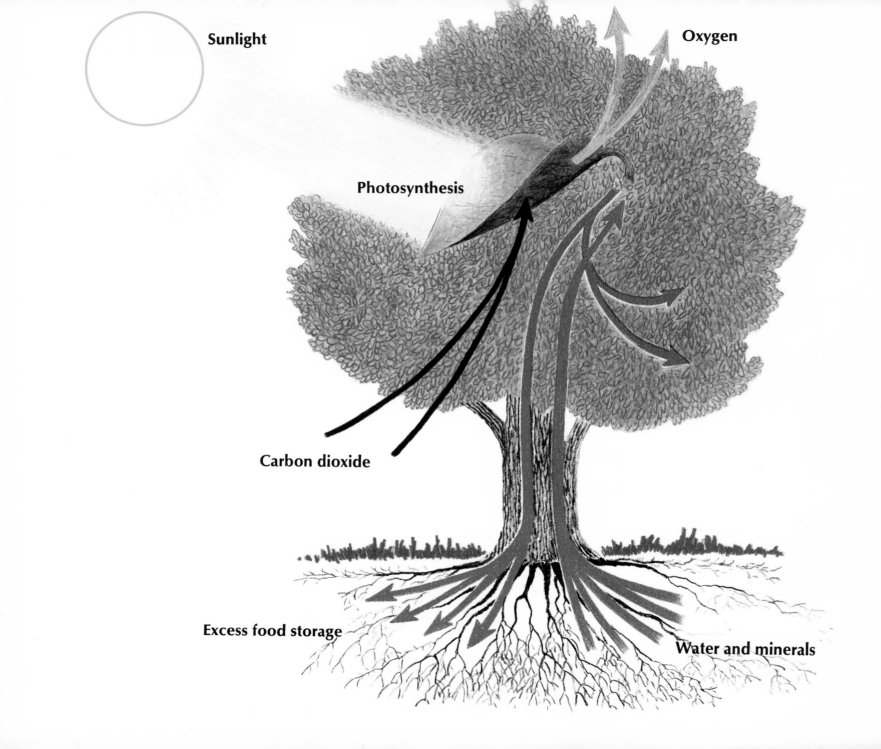

Sunlight

Oxygen

Photosynthesis

Carbon dioxide

Excess food storage

Water and minerals

1 Chemobacteria
50 species

4 Blue-green algae
1,500 species

7 Dinoflagellates
1,000 species

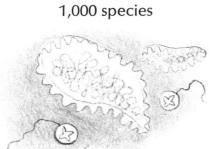

83828

2 Photobacteria
50 species

8 Guglenoids
450 species

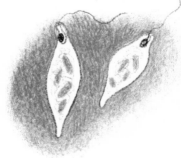

3 Staph, bacilli, etc.
2,000 species

9 Fungi
40,000 species